GUESS THE ANIMALS!
BY NIKI NAGHASH
I0837571

I AM ONE OF THE LARGEST AND MOST POWERFUL CATS IN THE WORLD, KNOWN FOR MY BEAUTIFUL ORANGE COAT AND DISTINCTIVE STRIPES. I'M A FIERCE PREDATOR, AND MY SHARP CLAWS AND TEETH MAKE ME A FORMIDABLE HUNTER. WHO AM I?

A TIGER!

I AM THE TALLEST MAMMAL IN THE WORLD, WITH A LONG NECK AND LEGS THAT ALLOW ME TO REACH THE LEAVES AT THE TOPS OF TREES. MY SPOTS ARE AS UNIQUE AS HUMAN FINGERPRINTS, AND I'M KNOWN FOR MY CALM AND GENTLE NATURE. WHO AM I?

A GIRAFFE!

I AM ONE OF THE LARGEST LAND ANIMALS IN THE WORLD, WITH A LONG TRUNK THAT I USE TO DRINK, EAT, AND COMMUNICATE WITH OTHERS. MY TUSKS ARE ACTUALLY LONG TEETH, AND I USE THEM FOR DEFENSE AND FORAGING. WHO AM I?

AN ELEPHANT!

I AM A LARGE REPTILE THAT LIVES IN AND AROUND BODIES OF WATER. MY POWERFUL JAWS AND SHARP TEETH MAKE ME A FEARSOME PREDATOR, AND MY ARMORED SKIN PROTECTS ME FROM ATTACKS. WHO AM I?

A CROCODILE!

I AM A HIGHLY INTELLIGENT MARINE MAMMAL, KNOWN FOR MY ACROBATIC DISPLAYS AND SOCIAL NATURE. I COMMUNICATE WITH OTHERS USING A VARIETY OF CLICKS AND WHISTLES, AND I CAN SWIM AT SPEEDS OF UP TO 60 KILOMETERS PER HOUR. WHO AM I?

A DOLPHIN!

I AM A LARGE, POWERFUL MAMMAL THAT HAS BEEN DOMESTICATED BY HUMANS FOR THOUSANDS OF YEARS. I'M KNOWN FOR MY SPEED AND ENDURANCE, AND MY STRONG SOCIAL BONDS WITH OTHER HORSES. WHO AM I?

A HORSE!

I AM A MARSUPIAL THAT LIVES IN AUSTRALIA, KNOWN FOR MY POWERFUL LEGS AND ABILITY TO HOP LONG DISTANCES. MY POUCH ALLOWS ME TO CARRY MY YOUNG WITH ME AS I MOVE AROUND. WHO AM I?

A KANGAROO!

I AM A MARSUPIAL THAT LIVES IN EUCALYPTUS TREES IN AUSTRALIA. MY DIET CONSISTS ALMOST ENTIRELY OF EUCALYPTUS LEAVES, AND I SPEND MOST OF MY DAY SLEEPING OR LOUNGING IN THE TREES. WHO AM I?

A KOALA!

I AM A LARGE CAT THAT LIVES IN THE GRASSLANDS OF AFRICA. I'M KNOWN FOR MY DISTINCTIVE ROAR AND MY ABILITY TO HUNT IN GROUPS. WHO AM I?

A LION!

I AM A LARGE, POWERFUL MAMMAL THAT LIVES IN A VARIETY OF HABITATS AROUND THE WORLD. I'M KNOWN FOR MY LOVE OF HONEY AND MY ABILITY TO HIBERNATE THROUGH THE WINTER MONTHS. WHO AM I?

A BEAR!

I AM A LARGE, HERBIVOROUS MAMMAL THAT LIVES IN THE GRASSLANDS OF AFRICA. MY DISTINCTIVE STRIPES MAKE ME EASY TO SPOT, AND I'M KNOWN FOR MY SPEED AND AGILITY. WHO AM I?

A ZEBRA!

I AM A LARGE, POWERFUL MAMMAL THAT LIVES IN AFRICA AND ASIA. MY THICK SKIN PROTECTS ME FROM PREDATORS, AND MY HORN IS ACTUALLY MADE OF KERATIN, THE SAME MATERIAL AS HUMAN HAIR AND NAILS. WHO AM I?

A RHINO!

I AM A HIGHLY INTELLIGENT SEA CREATURE WITH EIGHT TENTACLES AND A SOFT BODY. I'M KNOWN FOR MY ABILITY TO CHANGE COLOR AND SHAPE TO BLEND IN WITH MY SURROUNDINGS, AND MY BEAK IS STRONG ENOUGH TO CRACK OPEN SHELLS. WHO AM I?

AN OCTOPUS!

I AM A LEGLESS REPTILE THAT LIVES IN A VARIETY OF HABITATS AROUND THE WORLD. I'M KNOWN FOR MY ABILITY TO SWALLOW PREY WHOLE AND MY ABILITY TO SHED MY SKIN AS I GROW. WHO AM I?

A SNAKE!

I AM A NOCTURNAL BIRD OF PREY, KNOWN FOR MY SILENT FLIGHT AND ACUTE HEARING. I CAN ROTATE MY HEAD ALMOST ALL THE WAY AROUND, AND MY SHARP TALONS MAKE ME A SKILLED HUNTER. WHO AM I?

AN OWL!

THE END